How to Pray the Rosary
as a Pathway
to Contemplation

How to Pray the Rosary as a Pathway to Contemplation

Kathryn Marcellino

Lighthouse Publishing

HOW TO PRAY THE ROSARY
AS A PATHWAY TO CONTEMPLATION
by Kathryn Marcellino

Cover design and graphic design by Kathryn Marcellino. The art masterpieces used for each mystery are from the public domain with the framed borders added to them.

The scripture quotations are from The Challoner Revision of the Douay-Rheims Bible and the World English Bible, both in the public domain.

Library of Congress Control Number: 2005935188

Lighthouse Publishing
PO Box 40
Gladstone, Oregon 97027
(503) 655-3374

www.CatholicSpiritualDirection.org

ISBN: 0-945272-26-X
13-digit ISBN: 978-0-945272-26-7

Table of Contents

*This book is dedicated to
the honor and glory of God,
to our Blessed Mother, Mary,
and to my family.*

Introduction

It is marvelous to see the fruits of prayer in someone's life. In the life of Pope John Paul II, we have learned much about his love for the rosary, especially in his Apostolic Letter *The Rosary of the Blessed Virgin Mary*. Kathryn Marcellino has written this little book as part of the fruits of her own prayer.

Kathryn loves the rosary very much and wants to share that love with others. To do that, she has compiled this attractive little book which will hopefully lead many others to love Jesus and Mary more. Her thoughts and the art work she has selected have helped inspire me to pray. May this book do the same for you!

Fr. Donald Kinney, O.C.D.
Rector, Carmelite House of Studies
Mt. Angel, Oregon

The Rosary,
A Contemplative Prayer

"The Rosary, precisely because it starts with Mary's own experience, is an exquisitely contemplative prayer . . . By its nature the recitation of the Rosary calls for a quiet rhythm and a lingering pace, helping the individual to meditate on the mysteries of the Lord's life as seen through the eyes of her who was closest to the Lord. In this way the unfathomable riches of these mysteries are disclosed." – *from Pope John Paul II's Apostolic Letter on the Rosary of the Virgin Mary (Rosarium Virginis Mariae)*

A Pathway to Contemplation
❧

God is love. He loves us and desires that we love him in return. Prayer is how we interact and communicate with God. The purpose of prayer is to have a personal loving relationship with God. One excellent way that we can increase our knowledge and of love of God is through praying the rosary.

This book is written to help you pray the rosary as it is meant to be prayed: as a meditation on Gospel events from the lives of Jesus and Mary. It contains instructions on how to say the prayers of the rosary, how to meditate on the mysteries and how to pray the rosary in a way to remain receptive to God's actions during prayer so that it becomes a "pathway to contemplation".

The main part of the book includes Scripture passages and art masterpieces for each mystery to use as a visual aid while praying the rosary. It also includes information on the prayer of contemplation and how to recognize the transition from meditation to contemplation. There are also chapters on loving God, making progress in prayer and tips on saying a family rosary with children.

The reflections in the book come from the practice of daily prayer, and from the study of Church teachings, the writings of the Saints and Carmelite spirituality.

Pope John Paul II in his Apostolic Letter, *The Rosary of the Virgin Mary*, said, "The Rosary of the Virgin Mary, which gradually took form in the second millennium under the guidance of the Spirit of God, is a prayer loved by countless Saints and encouraged by the Magisterium. Simple yet profound, it still remains, at the dawn of this third millennium, a prayer of great significance, destined to bring forth a harvest of holiness."

The rosary as a meditative prayer

Many people think of the rosary as merely reciting a number of vocal prayers on beads. While vocal prayer has a value in itself (when we think about the words and open our minds and hearts to God), the rosary is meant to be much more than a recitation of vocal prayers. It is meant to be a meditation on important events called "mysteries" in the life of Jesus and his mother. In this way the rosary is joining with Mary, the mother of Jesus, to ponder in the depths of our heart the same mysteries that Mary pondered and experienced in her life through her relationship with her Son. Such meditation helps us to get to know Jesus and Mary better and to love them more and more.

At Fatima, Portugal in 1917, Mary appeared to three children, Lucia, Francisco and Jacinta and said, "Pray the rosary every day." Lucia said, "My impression is that Our Lady wanted to give ordinary people, who might not know how to pray, this simple method of getting closer to God." Mary taught seven-year old Jacinta how to meditate on the mysteries of the rosary by forming images of the mysteries in her mind as she prayed the Hail Marys.

Meditation is a mental prayer which seeks to make real to our minds and heart the things upon which we meditate, think about and ponder.

The *Catechism of the Catholic Church* (#2708) says, "Meditation engages thought, imagination, emotion, and desire. This mobilization of faculties is necessary in order to deepen our convictions of faith, prompt the conversion of our heart, and strengthen our will to follow Christ. Christian prayer tries above all to meditate on the mysteries of Christ, as in *Lectio Divina* or the rosary. This form of prayerful reflection is of great value, but Christian prayer should go further: to the knowledge of the love of the Lord Jesus, to union with him."

The prayer of contemplation

Contemplation is considered the highest form of prayer and goes beyond meditating on the things of God. It is a prayer more given to us by God than something we bring about. It is sometimes called a loving gaze on God or an experience of God or mystical prayer.

In contemplation we may also realize something about God or ourselves not resulting from our own reasoning, but because God gives us the realization and impresses it upon us. The intensity of contemplation can vary from slight to absorbing and from a shorter to longer duration over time.

Fr. Thomas Dubay in his book, *Fire Within,* describes contemplation as "a divinely originated, general, nonconceptual, loving awareness of God. At times this is a delightful, loving attention, at times a dry purifying desire, at times a strong thirsting for him."

He says that contemplation transforms a person and, if all goes well, leads to transforming union (also called spiritual marriage), which is the highest stage of spiritual development possible on earth.

Contemplation is a prayer that God initiates, not something we bring about through learning or practicing a certain technique. There are things we can learn and do, though, to help make ourselves receptive to contemplation and to recognize it in its subtle beginnings.

Even if we are not yet given this gift of contemplation, there is still much to be gained from meditation.

In mental prayer and meditation we come to know Jesus and Mary better by thinking about them and their lives. This helps us to love them more. We learn by their words and example how to live our lives more fully in tune with God and his will and plan for us. Thus meditation can become a pathway to contemplation.

For more about contemplation, including information on the transition from meditation to contemplation, refer to the chapter, "Making Progress in Prayer", toward the end of this book.

How To Use This Book

The book is meant to be an instruction on how to pray the rosary as it is meant to be prayed. So with that in mind it is suggested that you read this short chapter and then begin to pray the rosary or part of the rosary every day. Then, as you have time, read the other sections of the book for further instruction. The important thing is to begin to pray, and not only read about it. Prayer is meant to develop our relationship with God and the practice and experience of prayer is how we communicate with God in order to build that loving relationship.

The rosary is a form of prayer that is highly recommended for everyone, from beginners in prayer to the most advanced. It is made up of twenty decades of ten Hail Marys with an Our Father and Glory Be between each one. Usually we say five decades at a time meditating on one set of mysteries, i.e. the Joyful, Sorrowful, Luminous or Glorious mysteries.

The next section of this book has instructions on how to say the prayers of the rosary. Following that is the main part of this book, which is meant to be used time and time again. It is a Scriptural and visual aid to use while praying the rosary.

Prayer is mainly learned by doing, not by reading about it, even though some instruction is necessary. So why not begin today? Just like learning to play a musical instrument, the notes are all on the page, but it takes practice to make them sound like music. In a sense, prayer is like a skill or an art. We can learn the mechanics, but we don't become good at it unless we practice. The more we practice, the better we become. As we do what we can, God gives us his grace and makes up for our defects. "Taste and see the goodness of the Lord" (Psalm 33:8) by jumping right in and beginning to pray. Make prayer a priority by setting aside a time to pray each day.

Preparation for prayer

Decide on a good time and place for prayer in order to have minimal outer distractions. Experiment to see what works best for you and your circumstances.

Before beginning to pray the rosary, take a few moments to recollect yourself. This means to put yourself in the presence of God as best as you can mentally and emotionally. Set aside all your other concerns by giving them all to God. The Bible says, "Cast all your cares on him because he cares for you." (1 Peter 5:7) and "Be anxious for nothing." (Phil 4:6). Jesus desires that we have his peace.

Let God be God

If you start to pray and you are distracted by worries and concerns, one idea is to consciously bring what is on your mind to God in prayer. A way to do this is to visualize putting each concern into God's hands one by one. For example, if you are worried about money, visualize actually putting your financial situation into God hands and say, "Jesus, I trust in you. Show me what I should do and help me to do it," or words to that effect.

Ask for what you need and trust God to take care of you as he promised to do in the Bible if you "seek first" his kingdom. (See Matt 6:33.) To pray for loved ones, visualize putting each of them into God's hands in the same way, and so on for all your concerns. God requires that we make an effort, but he promises to help us and make up for our lack.

At times we may be tempted to try to tell God how to do things or even beg him for things, but we need to put it in his hands and trust that he will take care of things in the best way and at the best time. It doesn't make sense to try to manage God. We need to let God be in control and let God be God. Mother Teresa of Calcutta suggested that we let God show us what he can do.

The Bible says, "Until now you have not asked anything in my name; ask and you will receive, so that your joy may be complete." (John 16:24) When asking, let's keep in mind that God knows what is best for us. It is a good idea to add, "if it be in accordance with your will" or "not my will but yours be done" (Luke 22:42) to all our petitions.

In prayer, we come before the King of the Universe. Jesus invites us to ask and we shall receive, so why not ask for important things? We can ask God to bless us according to his riches and glory and not as we deserve. We can ask for things that really matter, like spiritual riches. We can strive to become a Saint and not just to squeak through the door of purgatory at the last minute make it to the very last place in Heaven. We can set our standards high because "we can do all things in God who strengthens us."

There's a saying that we better be careful about what we pray for, because we might get it. Sometimes we might try to convince God to do things our way, but it is wiser to seek God's way and plan and ask for things on the condition they will be good for us and others. The Bible says to persevere in prayer. God knows and desires what is best for us. He hears our prayers and answers them in His timing. It has been said that prayer doesn't change God, it changes us. Our goal should be to become more like God, not that God be more like us.

Meditating on the mysteries of the rosary

Prayer is a communication between God and us. Our part in praying the rosary is to say the vocal prayers and to meditate (think about or dwell) on the mystery for each decade. The mysteries are events from the life of Jesus and Mary. The Joyful Mysteries are about Jesus' conception, birth and childhood; the Luminous Mysteries about his public ministry; the Sorrowful Mysteries about his passion and death; and the Glorious Mysteries about events after his death.

When we meditate on the mysteries, we visualize or think about some of the main events from the lives of Jesus and Mary from the Bible. Each mystery has a message and meaning for our own life and our relationship with God.

In prayer, God is very present and right there with us. The more we pray with the desire to hear God, the more we develop an inner ear to hear him. As we meditate on the mysteries, we put our inner focus on God and can expect that ultimately he will be our guide and bring us closer to himself.

To really love God or anyone else, first you have to get to know them. You can't love what you don't know. Meditating on the mysteries of the rosary is a way to get to know Jesus and Mary better and therefore to love them more. It is more than an exercise of the mind and is not an emptying of the mind. Rather it is a refocusing of the mind from the outer realities to inner and spiritual ones. As we meditate on the mysteries of the rosary, thoughts and then sentiments are generated. We lift these to the Lord as part of our prayer. In this way meditation becomes not only a mental prayer but becomes an "affective" prayer, which means a prayer that engages our emotions as well.

In reflecting on the mysteries and opening our hearts to God, we begin to have more sentiments of love, praise, thanksgiving and intercession for others. We lift up our thoughts, intentions and feelings. Even if these remain unspoken, God reads our minds and hearts. As time goes on, God makes his presence known more and more and our relationship to God grows closer. This is perhaps why Pope John Paul II called the rosary "a path to contemplation".

Using this book as an aid in meditation

For each mystery, this book has a visual representation from an art masterpiece and a Scriptural or other passage for reflection. Meditating on the Scripture and the artwork helps us to better understand and visualize the Gospel event.

One way to use this book as a help to praying the rosary is to say the beginning six prayers of the rosary while paying attention to the meaning of the words. We begin the rosary by saying The Apostle's Creed which contains the basic truths of our faith. Then we say the Our Father which is the prayer Jesus taught us to pray. Following this we say three Hail Mary's in honor of Mary and to ask her to pray for us. Then we say the Glory Be which is a prayer of praise to God.

Next we announce the first mystery, for example we could say, "The first Joyful Mystery is the Annunciation". At this time we may change our focus from thinking about the meaning of the words of each of the prayers to thinking about the meaning of the mystery for that decade. So while we say the Our Father, 10 Hail Marys and Glory Be for the decade, we meditate on the mystery that we just announced.

An idea for using this book to help meditate on the mysteries, is to begin the decade by announcing the mystery. Pray the Our Father. Then take time to read some or all of the Scripture passage in this book for the specific mystery. While saying the 10 Hail Marys, think about the meaning of the words from the Scripture passage and let them soak in. Or perhaps focus on a certain idea or phrase from the Scripture passage that particularly strikes you. And so on for the rest of the decades.

Some ways to meditate on the mysteries are to imagine yourself as actually present at the event or to think about what the Bible is teaching in the passage. What does God wish to communicate to us? What did Jesus and Mary do and say? What might they have felt? What would we feel if we were one of the actual witnesses or participants?

The mysteries contain important lessons for us and show us ways to conform our lives more closely to God's will and plan. Keep in mind that God is always near and enlightens us in prayer, so open your mind and heart to him.

Practice and persevere

It is sometimes said that one should "pray as you can and not as you can't." Experiment to see what works best for you. Prayer is learned in the doing, so the important thing is to begin and to persevere. As we persevere in praying the rosary, Jesus, Mary and the events from the Gospels upon which we meditate will become more real to us.

St. Teresa of Avila said the path to union with God is prayer. Begin (again) on this path today with a "very determined determination", as she advises, and continue until you pass the finish line. Your reward will be the Lord giving himself to you as you give yourself to him. There is no greater thing that God can give you than himself.

How to Pray the Rosary

Say 10 Hail Marys,
while meditating
on the 3rd Mystery

Say a Glory Be,
(Optional Fatima Prayer),
Announce the 4th
Mystery, Our Father

Say 10 Hail Marys,
while meditating
on the 4th Mystery

Say a Glory Be,
(Optional Fatima Prayer),
Announce 5th
Mystery, Our Father

Say 10 Hail Marys,
while meditating
on the 5th Mystery

End with a Glory Be,
(Optional Fatima Prayer),
Hail Holy Queen and
the Ending Prayers

Say a Glory Be,
(Optional Fatima Prayer),
Announce the 3rd
Mystery, Our Father

Say 10 Hail Marys,
while meditating
on 2nd Mystery

Say a Glory Be,
(Optional Fatima Prayer),
Announce 2nd
Mystery, Our Father

Say 10 Hail Marys,
while meditating
on 1st Mystery

Say a Glory Be,
Announce 1st Mystery,
and the Our Father

Say 3 Hail Marys

Say an Our Father

Begin here with the
Sign of the Cross and
the Apostles Creed

Praying a rosary is usually understood to mean praying five decades at a time (one set of mysteries). The Joyful Mysteries are generally said on Monday and Saturday, the Luminous on Thursday, the Sorrowful on Tuesday and Friday and the Glorious on Wednesday and Sunday. (Exceptions: The Joyful on Sundays of Christmas Season and the Sorrowful on Sundays of Lent.)

The Prayers of the Rosary

Sign of the Cross

In the name of the Father, and of the Son and of the Holy Spirit. Amen.

Apostles' Creed

I believe in God, the Father almighty, Creator of Heaven and Earth; and in Jesus Christ, His only Son, our Lord; Who was conceived by the Holy Spirit, born of the Virgin Mary, suffered under Pontius Pilate, was crucified, died and was buried. He descended into hell. On the third day He rose again. He ascended into Heaven and is seated at the right hand of God, the Father almighty. From thence He will come again to judge the living and the dead. I believe in the Holy Spirit, the holy catholic Church, the communion of saints, the forgiveness of sins, the resurrection of the body, and life everlasting. Amen.

Our Father

Our Father, Who art in Heaven, Hallowed be Thy Name. Thy Kingdom come, Thy will be done on earth as it is in Heaven. Give us this day our daily bread, and forgive us our trespasses as we forgive those who trespass against us. And lead us not into temptation, but deliver us from evil. Amen.

Glory Be

Glory be to the Father and to the Son and to the Holy Spirit, As it was in the beginning, is now and ever shall be, world without end. Amen.

Hail Mary

Hail Mary, full of grace, the Lord is with thee. Blessed art thou among women, and blessed is the fruit of thy womb, Jesus. Holy Mary, Mother of God, pray for us sinners now and at the hour of our death. Amen.

Fatima Prayer

Oh my Jesus, forgive us our sins, save us from the fires of hell; lead all souls to Heaven, especially those most in need of Your Mercy.

Hail, Holy Queen

Hail, holy Queen, Mother of Mercy! Our life, our sweetness, and our hope! To thee do we cry, poor banished children of Eve, to thee do we send up our sighs, mourning and weeping in this valley, of tears. Turn, then, most gracious advocate, thine eyes of mercy toward us; and after this our exile show unto us the blessed fruit of thy womb Jesus; O clement, O loving, O sweet virgin Mary.

Ending Prayers

Pray for us, O holy Mother of God.
That we may be made worthy of the promises of Christ.

Let us pray. O God, whose only begotten Son, by His life, death, and resurrection, has purchased for us the rewards of eternal life, grant, we beseech Thee, that meditating upon these mysteries of the Most Holy Rosary of the Blessed Virgin Mary, we may imitate what they contain and obtain what they promise, through the same Christ Our Lord. Amen.

The following pages are meant to be
used while praying the rosary.
One way to do this is to read part or all
of the Scripture passage for each mystery
before starting each decade. Then look
at the artwork while praying the ten
Hail Marys to help you visualize the
mystery you are meditating upon.

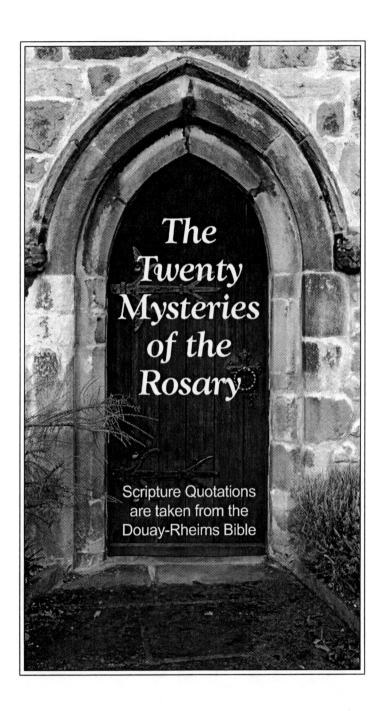

The Twenty Mysteries of the Rosary

Scripture Quotations are taken from the Douay-Rheims Bible

The Joyful Mysteries

The First Joyful Mystery
The Annunciation

Luke 1: 21-38

21 And the people were waiting for Zachary: and they wondered that he tarried so long in the temple.

22 And when he came out, he could not speak to them: and they understood that he had seen a vision in the temple. And he made signs to them and remained dumb.

23 And it came to pass, after the days of his office were accomplished, he departed to his own house.

24 And after those days, Elizabeth his wife conceived and hid herself five months, saying:

25 Thus hath the Lord dealt with me in the days wherein he hath had regard to take away my reproach among men.

26 And in the sixth month, the angel Gabriel was sent from God into a city of Galilee, called Nazareth,

27 To a virgin espoused to a man whose name was Joseph, of the house of David: and the virgin's name was Mary.

28 And the angel being come in, said unto her: Hail, full of grace, the Lord is with thee: blessed art thou among women.

29 Who having heard, was troubled at his saying and thought with herself what manner of salutation this should be.

30 And the angel said to her: Fear not, Mary, for thou hast found grace with God.

31 Behold thou shalt conceive in thy womb and shalt bring forth a son: and thou shalt call his name Jesus.

32 He shall be great and shall be called the Son of the Most High. And the Lord God shall give unto him the throne of David his father: and he shall reign in the house of Jacob for ever.

33 And of his kingdom there shall be no end.

34 And Mary said to the angel: How shall this be done, because I know not man?

35 And the angel answering, said to her: The Holy Ghost shall come upon thee and the power of the Most High shall overshadow thee. And therefore also the Holy which shall be born of thee shall be called the Son of God.

36 And behold thy cousin Elizabeth, she also hath conceived a son in her old age: and this is the sixth month with her that is called barren.

37 Because no word shall be impossible with God.

38 And Mary said: Behold the handmaid of the Lord: be it done to me according to thy word. And the angel departed from her.

The Second Joyful Mystery
The Visitation

Luke 1: 39-60

39 And Mary rising up in those days, went into the hill country with haste into a city of Juda.

40 And she entered into the house of Zachary and saluted Elizabeth.

41 And it came to pass that when Elizabeth heard the salutation of Mary, the infant leaped in her womb. And Elizabeth was filled with the Holy Ghost.

42 And she cried out with a loud voice and said: Blessed art thou among women and blessed is the fruit of thy womb.

43 And whence is this to me that the mother of my Lord should come to me?

44 For behold as soon as the voice of thy salutation sounded in my ears, the infant in my womb leaped for joy.

45 And blessed art thou that hast believed, because those things shall be accomplished that were spoken to thee by the Lord.

46 And Mary said: My soul doth magnify the Lord.

47 And my spirit hath rejoiced in God my Saviour.

48 Because he hath regarded the humility of his handmaid: for behold from henceforth all generations shall call me blessed.

49 Because he that is mighty hath done great things to me: and holy is his name.

50 And his mercy is from generation unto generations, to them that fear him.

51 He hath shewed might in his arm: he hath scattered the proud in the conceit of their heart.

52 He hath put down the mighty from their seat and hath exalted the humble.

53 He hath filled the hungry with good things: and the rich he hath sent empty away.

54 He hath received Israel his servant, being mindful of his mercy.

55 As he spoke to our fathers: to Abraham and to his seed for ever.

56 And Mary abode with her about three months. And she returned to her own house.

57 Now Elizabeth's full time of being delivered was come: and she brought forth a son.

58 And her neighbors and kinsfolks heard that the Lord had shewed his great mercy towards her: and they congratulated with her.

59 And it came to pass that on the eighth day they came to circumcise the child: and they called him by his father's name Zachary.

60 And his mother answering, said: Not so. But he shall be called John.

The Third Joyful Mystery
The Nativity

Luke 2: 1-20

1 And it came to pass that in those days there went out a decree from Caesar Augustus that the whole world should be enrolled.

2 This enrolling was first made by Cyrinus, the governor of Syria.

3 And all went to be enrolled, every one into his own city.

4 And Joseph also went up from Galilee, out of the city of Nazareth, into Judea, to the city of David, which is called Bethlehem: because he was of the house and family of David.

5 To be enrolled with Mary his espoused wife, who was with child.

6 And it came to pass that when they were there, her days were accomplished that she should be delivered.

7   And she brought forth her first born son and wrapped
     him up in swaddling clothes and laid him in a manger:
     because there was no room for them in the inn.

8   And there were in the same country shepherds watch-
     ing and keeping the night watches over their flock.

9   And behold an angel of the Lord stood by them and
     the brightness of God shone round about them: and
     they feared with a great fear.

10   And the angel said to them: Fear not; for, behold, I
     bring you good tidings of great joy that shall be to
     all the people:

11   For, this day is born to you a Saviour, who is Christ
     the Lord, in the city of David.

12   And this shall be a sign unto you. You shall find the
     infant wrapped in swaddling clothes and laid in a manger.

13   And suddenly there was with the angel a multitude
     of the heavenly army, praising God and saying:

14   Glory to God in the highest: and on earth peace to
     men of good will.

15   And it came to pass, after the angels departed from
     them into heaven, the shepherds said one to another:
     Let us go over to Bethlehem and let us see this word
     that is come to pass, which the Lord hath shewed to us.

16   And they came with haste: and they found Mary
     and Joseph, and the infant lying in the manger.

17   And seeing, they understood of the word that had
     been spoken to them concerning this child.

18   And all that heard wondered: and at those things
     that were told them by the shepherds.

19   But Mary kept all these words, pondering them in
     her heart.

20   And the shepherds returned, glorifying and praising
     God for all the things they had heard and seen, as it
     was told unto them.

The Fourth Joyful Mystery
The Presentation

Luke 2: 21-39

21 And after eight days were accomplished, that the child should be circumcised, his name was called JESUS, which was called by the angel before he was conceived in the womb.

22 And after the days of her purification, according to the law of Moses, were accomplished, they carried him to Jerusalem, to present him to the Lord:

23 As it is written in the law of the Lord: Every male opening the womb shall be called holy to the Lord:

24 And to offer a sacrifice, according as it is written in the law of the Lord, a pair of turtledoves or two young pigeons:

25 And behold there was a man in Jerusalem named Simeon: and this man was just and devout, waiting for the consolation of Israel. And the Holy Ghost was in him.

26 And he had received an answer from the Holy
Ghost, that he should not see death before he had
seen the Christ of the Lord.

27 And he came by the Spirit into the temple. And
when his parents brought in the child Jesus, to do
for him according to the custom of the law,

28 He also took him into his arms and blessed God
and said

29 Now thou dost dismiss thy servant, O Lord, according to thy word in peace:

30 Because my eyes have seen thy salvation,

31 Which thou hast prepared before the face of all
peoples:

32 A light to the revelation of the Gentiles and the
glory of thy people Israel.

33 And his father and mother were wondering at
those things which were spoken concerning him.

34 And Simeon blessed them and said to Mary his
mother: Behold this child is set for the fall and for
the resurrection of many in Israel and for a sign
which shall be contradicted.

35 And thy own soul a sword shall pierce, that, out of
many hearts thoughts may be revealed.

36 And there was one Anna, a prophetess, the daugh-
ter of Phanuel, of the tribe of Aser. She was far
advanced in years and had lived with her husband
seven years from her virginity.

37 And she was a widow until fourscore and four
years: who departed not from the temple, by
fastings and prayers serving night and day.

38 Now she, at the same hour, coming in, confessed
to the Lord: and spoke of him to all that looked for
the redemption of Israel.

39 And after they had performed all things according
to the law of the Lord, they returned into Galilee,
to their city Nazareth.

The Fifth Joyful Mystery
The Finding of the Child Jesus in the Temple

Luke 2: 40-52

40 And the child grew and waxed strong, full of wisdom: and the grace of God was in him.

41 And his parents went every year to Jerusalem, at the solemn day of the pasch.

42 And when he was twelve years old, they going up into Jerusalem, according to the custom of the feast,

43 And having fulfilled the days, when they returned, the child Jesus remained in Jerusalem. And his parents knew it not.

44 And thinking that he was in the company, they came a day's journey and sought him among their kinsfolks and acquaintance.

45 And not finding him, they returned into Jerusalem, seeking him.

46 And it came to pass, that, after three days, they found him in the temple, sitting in the midst of the doctors, hearing them and asking them questions.

47 And all that heard him were astonished at his wisdom and his answers.

48 And seeing him, they wondered. And his mother said to him: Son, why hast thou done so to us? Behold thy father and I have sought thee sorrowing.

49 And he said to them: How is it that you sought me? Did you not know that I must be about my father's business?

50 And they understood not the word that he spoke unto them.

51 And he went down with them and came to Nazareth and was subject to them. And his mother kept all these words in her heart.

52 And Jesus advanced in wisdom and age and grace with God and men.

The Luminous Mysteries

Also known as "The Mysteries of Light".

The First Luminous Mystery
The Baptism of Jesus in the Jordan

Mark 1: 1-18

1   The beginning of the Gospel of Jesus Christ, the Son of God.
2   As it is written in Isaias the prophet: Behold I send my angel before thy face, who shall prepare the way before thee.
3   A voice of one crying in the desert: Prepare ye the way of the Lord; make straight his paths.
4   John was in the desert, baptizing and preaching the baptism of penance, unto remission of sins.
5   And there went out to him all the country of Judea and all they of Jerusalem and were baptized by him in the river of Jordan, confessing their sins.

6 And John was clothed camel's hair, and a leathern girdle about his loins: and he ate locusts and wild honey.

7 And he preached, saying: There cometh after me one mightier than I, the latchet of whose shoes I am not worthy to stoop down and loose.

8 I have baptized you with water: but he shall baptize you with the Holy Ghost.

9 And it came to pass, in those days, Jesus came from Nazareth of Galilee and was baptized by John in Jordan.

10 And forthwith coming up out of the water, he saw the heavens open and the Spirit as a dove descending and remaining on him.

11 And there came a voice from heaven: Thou art my beloved Son; in thee I am well pleased.

12 And immediately the Spirit drove him out into the desert.

13 And he was in the desert forty days and forty nights, and was tempted by Satan. And he was with beasts: and the angels ministered to him.

14 And after that John was delivered up, Jesus came in Galilee, preaching the Gospel of the kingdom of God,

15 And saying: The time is accomplished and the kingdom of God is at hand. Repent and believe the Gospel:

16 And passing by the sea of Galilee, he saw Simon and Andrew his brother, casting nets into the sea for they were fishermen.

17 And Jesus said to them: Come after me; and I will make you to become fishers of men.

18 And immediately leaving their nets, they followed him.

The Second Luminous Mystery
The Wedding Feast at Cana

John 2: 1-12

1   And the third day, there was a marriage in Cana of Galilee: and the mother of Jesus was there.

2   And Jesus also was invited, and his disciples, to the marriage.

3   And the wine failing, the mother of Jesus saith to him: They have no wine.

4   And Jesus saith to her: Woman, what is that to me and to thee? My hour is not yet come.

5   His mother saith to the waiters: Whatsoever he shall say to you, do ye.

6   Now there were set there six waterpots of stone, according to the manner of the purifying of the Jews, containing two or three measures apiece.

7   Jesus saith to them: Fill the waterpots with water. And they filled them up to the brim.

8   And Jesus saith to them: Draw out now and carry to the chief steward of the feast. And they carried it.

9   And when the chief steward had tasted the water made wine and knew not whence it was, but the waiters knew who had drawn the water: the chief steward calleth the bridegroom,

10   And saith to him: Every man at first setteth forth good wine, and when men have well drunk, then that which is worse. But thou hast kept the good wine until now.

11   This beginning of miracles did Jesus in Cana of Galilee and manifested his glory. And his disciples believed in him.

12   After this, he went down to Capharnaum, he and his mother and his brethren and his disciples: and they remained there not many days.

The Third Luminous Mystery
Proclamation of the Kingdom

Pope John Paul II in his Apostolic Letter on the Rosary of the Virgin Mary (*Rosarium Virginis Mariae*) said, "Another mystery of light is the preaching by which Jesus proclaims the coming of the Kingdom of God, calls to conversion (cf. Mk 1:15) and forgives the sins of all who draw near to him in humble trust (cf. Mk 2:3-13; Lk 7:47- 48): the inauguration of that ministry of mercy which he continues to exercise until the end of the world, particularly through the Sacrament of Reconciliation which he has entrusted to his Church (cf. Jn 20:22-23)."

Mark 1:15

1   And saying: The time is accomplished, and the kingdom of God is at hand: repent, and believe the gospel.

Mark 2:3-13

3 And they came to him, bringing one sick of the palsy, who was carried by four.

4 And when they could not offer him unto him for the multitude, they uncovered the roof where he was; and opening it, they let down the bed wherein the man sick of the palsy lay.

5 And when Jesus had seen their faith, he saith to the sick of the palsy: Son, thy sins are forgiven thee.

6 And there were some of the scribes sitting there, and thinking in their hearts:

7 Why doth this man speak thus? he blasphemeth. Who can forgive sins, but God only?

8 Which Jesus presently knowing in his spirit, that they so thought within themselves, saith to them: Why think you these things in your hearts?

9 Which is easier, to say to the sick of the palsy: Thy sins are forgiven thee; or to say: Arise, take up thy bed, and walk?

10 But that you may know that the Son of man hath power on earth to forgive sins, (he saith to the sick of the palsy,)

11 I say to thee: Arise, take up thy bed, and go into thy house.

12 And immediately he arose; and taking up his bed, went his way in the sight of all; so that all wondered and glorified God, saying: We never saw the like.

13 And he went forth again to the sea side; and all the multitude came to him, and he taught them.

Luke 7:47-48

47 Wherefore I say to thee: Many sins are forgiven her, because she hath loved much. But to whom less is forgiven, he loveth less.

48 And he said to her: Thy sins are forgiven thee.

John 20: 22-23

22 When he had said this, he breathed on them; and he said to them: Receive ye the Holy Ghost.

23 Whose sins you shall forgive, they are forgiven them; and whose sins you shall retain, they are retained.

The Fourth Luminous Mystery
The Transfiguration

Matt 17:1-13

1 And after six days Jesus taketh unto him Peter and James, and John his brother, and bringeth them up into a high mountain apart:

2 And he was transfigured before them. And his face did shine as the sun: and his garments became white as snow.

3 And behold there appeared to them Moses and Elias talking with him.

4 And Peter answering, said to Jesus: Lord, it is good for us to be here: if thou wilt, let us make here three tabernacles, one for thee, and one for Moses, and one for Elias.

5 And as he was yet speaking, behold a bright cloud overshadowed them. And lo a voice out of the cloud, saying: This is my beloved Son, in whom I am well pleased: hear ye him.

6 And the disciples hearing fell upon their face, and were very much afraid.

7 And Jesus came and touched them: and said to them: Arise, and fear not.

8 And they lifting up their eyes, saw no one, but only Jesus.

9 And as they came down from the mountain, Jesus charged them, saying: Tell the vision to no man, till the Son of man be risen from the dead.

10 And his disciples asked him, saying: Why then do the scribes say that Elias must come first?

11 But he answering, said to them: Elias indeed shall come, and restore all things.

12 But I say to you, that Elias is already come, and they knew him not, But have done unto him whatsoever they had a mind. So also the Son of man shall suffer from them.

13 Then the disciples understood, that he had spoken to them of John the Baptist.

The Fifth Luminous Mystery
Institution of the Eucharist

Matthew 26: 17-35

17   And on the first day of the Azymes, the disciples
came to Jesus, saying: Where wilt thou that we
prepare for thee to eat the pasch?

18   But Jesus said: Go ye into the city to a certain man
and say to him: The master saith, My time is near at
hand. With thee I make the pasch with my disciples.

19   And the disciples did as Jesus appointed to them:
and they prepared the pasch.

20   But when it was evening, he sat down with his
twelve disciples.

21   And whilst they were eating, he said: Amen I say
to you that one of you is about to betray me.

22   And they being very much troubled began every
one to say: Is it I, Lord?

23 But he answering said: He that dippeth his hand with me in the dish, he shall betray me.

24 The Son of man indeed goeth, as it is written of him. But woe to that man by whom the Son of man shall be betrayed. It were better for him, if that man had not been born.

25 And Judas that betrayed him answering, said: Is it I, Rabbi? He saith to him: Thou hast said it.

26 And whilst they were at supper, Jesus took bread and blessed and broke and gave to his disciples and said: Take ye and eat. This is my body.

27 And taking the chalice, he gave thanks and gave to them, saying: Drink ye all of this.

28 For this is my blood of the new testament, which shall be shed for many unto remission of sins.

29 And I say to you, I will not drink from henceforth of this fruit of the vine until that day when I shall drink it with you new in the kingdom of my Father.

30 And a hymn being said, they went out unto mount Olivet.

31 Then Jesus saith to them: All you shall be scandalized in me this night. For it is written: I will strike the shepherd: and the sheep of the flock shall be dispersed.

32 But after I shall be risen again, I will go before you into Galilee.

33 And Peter answering, said to him: Although all shall be scandalized in thee, I will never be scandalized.

34 Jesus said to him: Amen I say to thee that in this night before the cock crow, thou wilt deny me thrice.

35 Peter saith to him: Yea, though I should die with thee, I will not deny thee. And in like manner said all the disciples.

The Mysteries of the Rosary

A Quick Reference

Scripture meditations continue on page 55.

Joyful Mysteries

1. The Annunciation

The Angel Gabriel announces to Mary that she will be the Mother of Jesus, the Messiah.

2. The Visitation

Mary goes to visit her cousin, Elizabeth, who is expecting a child in her old age. The child will be known as St. John the Baptist.

3. The Nativity

Jesus is born in a stable in Bethlehem, wrapped in swaddling clothes and laid in a manger because there is no room for the Holy Family at the inn.

4. The Presentation

Mary and Joseph take Jesus to the temple to present him to the Lord according to the Law of Moses.

5. The Finding of Jesus in the Temple

Mary and Joseph find the twelve year old Jesus in the midst of the teachers in the temple after 3 days of searching for him.

Luminous Mysteries

1. The Baptism of Jesus in the Jordan

Jesus is baptized by St. John the Baptist.

2. The Wedding Feast at Cana

Jesus performs his first public miracle by changing water into wine at the request of his mother.

3. The Proclamation of the Kingdom

Jesus goes about preaching the gospel, forgiving sins, healing the sick and working many miracles.

4. Transfiguration

Jesus takes Peter, James and John to a high mountain where they see his face glowing like the sun and his garments white as snow, while he speaks with Moses and Elijah.

5. The Institution of the Eucharist

At his last supper with the apostles before he dies, Jesus institutes the sacrament of the Eucharist and says, "Do this in remembrance of me."

Sorrowful Mysteries

1. The Agony in the Garden

Jesus foresees his coming crucifixion and prays repeatedly, "Father if it be your will take this cup from me, but not my will but thine be done."

2. The Scourging at the Pillar

Jesus is cruelly beaten and then handed over to be crucified.

3. The Crowning with Thorns

Jesus is crowned with thorns and mocked by the soldiers. They spit on him and strike him on the head saying, "Hail, King of the Jews."

4. The Carrying of the Cross

The soldiers force Jesus to carry his cross and he falls three times.

5. The Crucifixion

Jesus dies on the cross for our eternal salvation and he prays, "Father, forgive them, for they do not know what they do."

Glorious Mysteries

1. The Resurrection

Jesus rises from the dead on the third day after his death on the cross.

2. The Ascension

The disciples see Jesus taken up into heaven in the clouds to take his seat at the right hand of God the Father.

3. The Descent of the Holy Spirit

The Holy Spirit comes upon the disciples and Mary in the form of tongues of fire. The disciples begin to speak in foreign tongues and preach to the crowds.

4. The Assumption

Mary, who was conceived without original sin, is taken up body and soul into Heaven.

5. The Coronation

As the mother of Jesus Christ, the Son of God, Mary is crowned the Queen of Heaven, and takes her place above all the angels and the saints.

The Sorrowful Mysteries

The First Sorrowful Mystery
The Agony in the Garden

Matt 26: 36-46

36 Then Jesus came with them into a country place which is called Gethsemani. And he said to his disciples: Sit you here, till I go yonder and pray.

37 And taking with him Peter and the two sons of Zebedee, he began to grow sorrowful and to be sad.

38 Then he saith to them: My soul is sorrowful even unto death. Stay you here and watch with me.

39 And going a little further, he fell upon his face, praying and saying: My Father, if it be possible, let this chalice pass from me. Nevertheless, not as I will but as thou wilt.

40 And he cometh to his disciples and findeth them asleep. And he saith to Peter: What? Could you not watch one hour with me?

41 Watch ye: and pray that ye enter not into temptation. The spirit indeed is willing, but the flesh is weak.

42 Again the second time, he went and prayed, saying: My Father, if this chalice may not pass away, but I must drink it, thy will be done.

43 And he cometh again and findeth them sleeping: for their eyes were heavy.

44 And leaving them, he went again: and he prayed the third time, saying the selfsame word.

45 Then he cometh to his disciples and said to them: Sleep ye now and take your rest. Behold the hour is at hand: and the Son of man shall be betrayed into the hands of sinners.

46 Rise: let us go. Behold he is at hand that will betray me.

The Second Sorrowful Mystery
The Scourging at the Pillar

John 18: 28-40, 19:1

28 Then they led Jesus from Caiphas to the governor's hall. And it was morning: and they went not into the hall, that they might not be defiled, but that they might eat the pasch.

29 Pilate therefore went out to them, and said: What accusation bring you against this man?

30 They answered and said to him: If he were not a malefactor, we would not have delivered him up to thee.

31 Pilate therefore said to them: Take him you, and judge him according to your law. The Jews there-

fore said to him: It is not lawful for us to put any man to death.

32 That the word of Jesus might be fulfilled, which he said, signifying what death he should die.

33 Pilate therefore went into the hall again and called Jesus and said to him: Art thou the king of the Jews?

34 Jesus answered: Sayest thou this thing of thyself, or have others told it thee of me?

35 Pilate answered: Am I a Jew? Thy own nation and the chief priests have delivered thee up to me. What hast thou done?

36 Jesus answered: My kingdom is not of this world. If my kingdom were of this world, my servants would certainly strive that I should not be delivered to the Jews: but now my kingdom is not from hence.

37 Pilate therefore said to him: Art thou a king then? Jesus answered: Thou sayest that I am a king. For this was I born, and for this came I into the world; that I should give testimony to the truth. Every one that is of the truth heareth my voice.

38 Pilate saith to him: What is truth? And when he said this, he went out again to the Jews and saith to them: I find no cause in him.

39 But you have a custom that I should release one unto you at the Pasch. Will you, therefore, that I release unto you the king of the Jews?

40 Then cried they all again, saying: Not this man, but Barabbas. Now Barabbas was a robber.

1 Then therefore Pilate took Jesus and scourged him.

The Third Sorrowful Mystery
The Crowning with Thorns

Mark 15: 1-20

1   And straightway in the morning, the chief priests holding a consultation with the ancients and the scribes and the whole council, binding Jesus, led him away and delivered him to Pilate.

2   And Pilate asked him: Art thou the king of the Jews? But he answering, saith to him: Thou sayest it.

3   And the chief priests accused him in many things.

4   And Pilate again asked him, saying: Answerest thou nothing? Behold in how many things they accuse thee.

5   But Jesus still answered nothing: so that Pilate wondered.

6 Now on the festival day he was wont to release unto them one of the prisoners, whomsoever they demanded.

7 And there was one called Barabbas, who was put in prison with some seditious men, who in the sedition had committed murder.

8 And when the multitude was come up, they began to desire that he would do as he had ever done unto them.

9 And Pilate answered them and said: Will you that I release to you the king of the Jews?

10 For he knew that the chief priests had delivered him up out of envy.

11 But the chief priests moved the people, that he should rather release Barabbas to them.

12 And Pilate again answering, saith to them: What will you then that I do to the king of the Jews?

13 But they again cried out: Crucify him.

14 And Pilate saith to them: Why, what evil hath he done? But they cried out the more: Crucify him.

15 And so Pilate being willing to satisfy the people, released to them Barabbas: and delivered up Jesus, when he had scourged him, to be crucified.

16 And the soldiers led him away into the court of the palace: and they called together the whole band.

17 And they clothed him with purple: and, platting a crown of thorns, they put it upon him.

18 And they began to salute him: Hail, king of the Jews.

19 And they struck his head with a reed: and they did spit on him. And bowing their knees, they adored him.

20 And after they had mocked him, they took off the purple from him and put his own garments on him: and they led him out to crucify him.

The Fourth Sorrowful Mystery
The Carrying of the Cross

Luke 23: 13-32

13 And Pilate, calling together the chief priests and the magistrates and the people,

14 Said to them: You have presented unto me this man as one that perverteth the people. And behold I, having examined him before you, find no cause in this man, in those things wherein you accuse him.

15 No, nor Herod neither. For, I sent you to him: and behold, nothing worthy of death is done to him.

16 I will chastise him therefore and release him.

17 Now of necessity he was to release unto them one upon the feast day.

18 But the whole multitude together cried out, saying: Away with this man, and release unto us Barabbas:

19 Who, for a certain sedition made in the city and for a murder, was cast into prison.

20 And Pilate again spoke to them, desiring to release Jesus.

21 But they cried again, saying: Crucify him, Crucify him.

22 And he said to them the third time: Why, what evil hath this man done? I find no cause of death in him. I will chastise him therefore and let him go.

23 But they were instant with loud voices, requiring that he might be crucified. And their voices prevailed.

24 And Pilate gave sentence that it should be as they required.

25 And he released unto them him who for murder and sedition had been cast into prison, whom they had desired. But Jesus he delivered up to their will.

26 And as they led him away, they laid hold of one Simon of Cyrene, coming from the country; and they laid the cross on him to carry after Jesus.

27 And there followed him a great multitude of people and of women, who bewailed and lamented him.

28 But Jesus turning to them, said: Daughters of Jerusalem, weep not over me; but weep for yourselves and for your children.

29 For behold, the days shall come, wherein they will say: Blessed are the barren and the wombs that have not borne and the paps that have not given suck.

30 Then shall they begin to say to the mountains: Fall upon us. And to the hills: Cover us.

31 For if in the green wood they do these things, what shall be done in the dry?

32 And there were also two other malefactors led with him to be put to death.

The Fifth Sorrowful Mystery
The Crucifixion

Luke 23:33-53

33 And when they were come to the place which is called Calvary, they crucified him there: and the robbers, one on the right hand, and the other on the left.

34 And Jesus said: Father, forgive them, for they know not what they do. But they, dividing his garments, cast lots.

35 And the people stood beholding. And the rulers with them derided him, saying: He saved others: let him save himself, if he be Christ, the elect of God.

36 And the soldiers also mocked him, coming to him and offering him vinegar,

37 And saying: If thou be the king of the Jews, save thyself.

38 And there was also a superscription written over him in letters of Greek and Latin and Hebrew THIS IS THE KING OF THE JEWS.

39 And one of those robbers who were hanged blasphemed him, saying: If thou be Christ, save thyself and us.

40 But the other answering, rebuked him, saying: Neither dost thou fear God, seeing; thou art under the same condemnation?

41 And we indeed justly: for we receive the due reward of our deeds. But this man hath done no evil.

42 And he said to Jesus: Lord, remember me when thou shalt come into thy kingdom.

43 And Jesus said to him: Amen I say to thee: This day thou shalt be with me in paradise.

44 And it was almost the sixth hour: and there was darkness over all the earth until the ninth hour.

45 And the sun was darkened, and the veil of the temple was rent in the midst.

46 And Jesus crying with a loud voice, said: Father, into thy hands I commend my spirit. And saying this, he gave up the ghost.

47 Now, the centurion, seeing what was done, glorified God, saying: Indeed this was a just man.

48 And all the multitude of them that were come together to that sight and saw the things that were done returned, striking their breasts.

49 And all his acquaintance and the women that had followed him from Galilee stood afar off, beholding these things.

50 And behold there was a man named Joseph who was a counsellor, a good and a just man,

51 (The same had not consented to their counsel and doings) of Arimathea, a city of Judea: who also himself looked for the kingdom of God.

52 This man went to Pilate and begged the body of Jesus.

53 And taking him down, he wrapped him in fine linen and laid him in a sepulchre that was hewed in stone, wherein never yet any man had been laid.

The Glorious Mysteries

The First Glorious Mystery
Resurrection from the Dead

Matt 28: 1-20

1   And in the end of the sabbath, when it began to dawn towards the first day of the week, came Mary Magdalen and the other Mary, to see the sepulchre.

2   And behold there was a great earthquake. For an angel of the Lord descended from heaven and coming rolled back the stone and sat upon it.

3   And his countenance was as lightning and his raiment as snow.

4   And for fear of him, the guards were struck with terror and became as dead men.

5   And the angel answering, said to the women: Fear not you: for I know that you seek Jesus who was crucified.

6   He is not here. For he is risen, as he said. Come, and see the place where the Lord was laid.

7   And going quickly, tell ye his disciples that he is risen. And behold he will go before you into Galilee. There you shall see him. Lo, I have foretold it to you.

8   And they went out quickly from the sepulchre with fear and great joy, running to tell his disciples.

9   And behold, Jesus met them, saying: All hail. But they came up and took hold of his feet and adored him.

10 Then Jesus said to them: Fear not. Go, tell my brethren that they go into Galilee. There they shall see me.

11 Who when they were departed, behold, some of the guards came into the city and told the chief priests all things that had been done.

12 And they being assembled together with the ancients, taking counsel, gave a great sum of money to the soldiers,

13 Saying: Say you, His disciples came by night and stole him away when we were asleep.

14 And if the governor shall hear of this, we will persuade him and secure you.

15 So they taking the money, did as they were taught: and this word was spread abroad among the Jews even unto this day.

16 And the eleven disciples went into Galilee, unto the mountain where Jesus had appointed them.

17 And seeing him they adored: but some doubted.

18 And Jesus coming, spoke to them, saying: All power is given to me in heaven and in earth.

19 Going therefore, teach ye all nations: baptizing them in the name of the Father and of the Son and of the Holy Ghost.

20 Teaching them to observe all things whatsoever I have commanded you. And behold I am with you all days, even to the consummation of the world.

The Second Glorious Mystery
The Ascension into Heaven

Acts 1: 1-12

1   The former treatise I made, O Theophilus, of all things which Jesus began to do and to teach,

2   Until the day on which, giving commandments by the Holy Ghost to the apostles whom he had chosen, he was taken up.

3   To whom also he shewed himself alive after his passion, by many proofs, for forty days appearing to them, and speaking of the kingdom of God.

4   And eating together with them, he commanded them, that they should not depart from Jerusalem, but should wait for the promise of the Father, which you have heard (saith he) by my mouth.

5   For John indeed baptized with water: but you shall be baptized with the Holy Ghost, not many days hence.

6   They therefore who were come together, asked him, saying: Lord, wilt thou at this time restore again the kingdom of Israel?

7   But he said to them: It is not for you to know the time or moments, which the Father hath put in his own power:

8   But you shall receive the power of the Holy Ghost coming upon you, and you shall be witnesses unto me in Jerusalem, and in all Judea, and Samaria, and even to the uttermost part of the earth.

9   And when he had said these things, while they looked on, he was raised up: and a cloud received him out of their sight.

10 And while they were beholding him going up to heaven, behold two men stood by them in white garments.

11 Who also said: Ye men of Galilee, why stand you looking up to heaven? This Jesus who is taken up from you into heaven, shall so come as you have seen him going into heaven.

12 Then they returned to Jerusalem from the mount that is called Olivet, which is nigh Jerusalem, within a sabbath day's journey.

The Third Glorious Mystery
Descent of the Holy Spirit

Acts 2: 1-18

1 And when the days of the Pentecost were accomplished, they were all together in one place:

2 And suddenly there came a sound from heaven, as of a mighty wind coming: and it filled the whole house where they were sitting.

3 And there appeared to them parted tongues, as it were of fire: and it sat upon every one of them.

4 And they were all filled with the Holy Ghost: and they began to speak with divers tongues, according as the Holy Ghost gave them to speak.

5 Now there were dwelling at Jerusalem, Jews, devout men, out of every nation under heaven.

6 And when this was noised abroad, the multitude came together, and were confounded in mind, because that every man heard them speak in his own tongue.

7 And they were all amazed, and wondered, saying: Behold, are not all these that speak Galilean?

8 And how have we heard, every man our own tongue wherein we were born?

9 Parthians and Medes and Elamites and inhabitants of Mesopotamia, Judea, and Cappadocia, Pontus and Asia,

10 Phrygia and Pamphylia, Egypt and the parts of Libya about Cyrene, and strangers of Rome,

11 Jews also, and proselytes, Cretes, and Arabians: we have heard them speak in our own tongues the wonderful works of God.

12 And they were all astonished, and wondered, saying one to another: What meaneth this?

13 But others mocking, said: These men are full of new wine.

14 But Peter standing up with the eleven, lifted up his voice, and spoke to them: Ye men of Judea, and all you that dwell in Jerusalem, be this known to you and with your ears receive my words.

15 For these are not drunk, as you suppose, seeing it is but the third hour of the day:

16 But this is that which was spoken of by the prophet Joel:

17 And it shall come to pass, in the last days, (saith the Lord), I will pour out of my Spirit upon all flesh: and your sons and your daughters shall prophesy: and your young men shall see visions, and your old men shall dream dreams.

18 And upon my servants indeed and upon my handmaids will I pour out in those days of my spirit: and they shall prophesy.

The Fourth Glorious Mystery
The Assumption of Mary

On November 1, 1950, Pius XII infallibly defined
the Assumption of Mary as a dogma of faith: "We pro-
nounce, declare and define it to be a divinely revealed
dogma that the immaculate Mother of God, the ever Virgin Mary, having completed the course of her earthly life,
was assumed body and soul to heavenly glory."

"Just as the Mother of Jesus, glorified in body and
soul in heaven, is the image and beginning of the Church
as it is to be perfected in the world to come, so too does
she shine forth on earth, until the day of the Lord shall
come, (2 Pet. 3:10) as a sign of sure hope and solace to
the people of God during its sojourn on earth." *From
Vatican II, Dogmatic Constitution on the Church, (68)*

"It was fitting that the she, who had kept her virginity intact in childbirth, should keep her own body free from all corruption even after death. It was fitting that she, who had carried the Creator as a child at her breast, should dwell in the divine tabernacles. It was fitting that the spouse, whom the Father had taken to himself, should live in the divine mansions. It was fitting that she, who had seen her Son upon the cross and who had thereby received into her heart the sword of sorrow which she had escaped when giving birth to him, should look upon him as he sits with the Father, It was fitting that God's Mother should possess what belongs to her Son, and that she should be honored by every creature as the Mother and as the handmaid of God." *St. John Damascene, Dormition of Mary [A.D. 697]*

Note: "But there are also many other things which Jesus did which, if they were written every one, the world itself, I think, would not be able to contain the books that should be written." *John 21:25.* The Assumption of Mary into Heaven and the Coronation of Mary (the fourth and fifth glorious mysteries) are not recorded in Scripture.

The Fifth Glorious Mystery
The Coronation of Mary as Queen of Heaven

"AD CAELI REGINAM",
Encyclical of Pope Pius XII
Proclaiming the Queenship of Mary
October 11, 1954

"From the earliest ages of the Catholic Church a Christian people, whether in time of triumph or more especially in time of crisis, has addressed prayers of petition and hymns of praise and veneration to the Queen of Heaven. And never has that hope wavered which they placed in the Mother of the Divine King, Jesus Christ; nor has that faith ever failed by which we are taught that Mary, the

Virgin Mother of God, reigns with a mother's solicitude over the entire world, just as she is crowned in heavenly blessedness with the glory of a Queen...

"38. From these considerations, the proof develops on these lines: if Mary, in taking an active part in the work of salvation, was, by God's design, associated with Jesus Christ, the source of salvation itself, in a manner comparable to that in which Eve was associated with Adam, the source of death, so that it may be stated that the work of our salvation was accomplished by a kind of 'recapitulation,'[49] in which a virgin was instrumental in the salvation of the human race, just as a virgin had been closely associated with its death; if, moreover, it can likewise be stated that this glorious Lady had been chosen Mother of Christ 'in order that she might become a partner in the redemption of the human race';[50] and if, in truth, 'it was she who, free of the stain of actual and original sin, and ever most closely bound to her Son, on Golgotha offered that Son to the Eternal Father together with the complete sacrifice of her maternal rights and maternal love, like a new Eve, for all the sons of Adam, stained as they were by his lamentable fall,'[51] then it may be legitimately concluded that as Christ, the new Adam, must be called a King not merely because He is Son of God, but also because He is our Redeemer, so, analogously, the Most Blessed Virgin is queen not only because she is Mother of God, but also because, as the new Eve, she was associated with the new Adam."

Why Pray the Rosary?

Jesus taught us that the two greatest commandments are to love the Lord, our God, with our whole heart, mind, soul and strength, and to love our neighbor as ourselves. Prayer helps us to come to that personal and deep love of God which also expresses itself in love of neighbor. Praying the rosary helps us to know Jesus more intimately and therefore to love him more. As we pray the rosary, we put our mind and hearts on God in various ways. Jesus Christ becomes more and more real to us as we ponder his life in the mysteries of the rosary.

The rosary not only helps us to have a closer relationship with God, but it can be offered as an intercessory prayer for others. Mary asked us at Fatima to pray the rosary for peace in the world, the salvation of souls, the conversion of sinners, and in reparation for sin. Mary is our mother who wants to bring us closer to her Son.

For beginners to advanced

The rosary can be said by everyone from beginners in the spiritual life to advanced, from small children to senior citizens, since it ranges from simple vocal prayers through meditation and all the way to contemplation. Mother Teresa of Calcutta, St. Padre Pio and Pope John Paul II prayed the rosary daily. The closer we come to God and the holier we become, the more effective our prayers will be, as we see in the lives of the Saints.

Sr. Lucia, one of the visionaries at Fatima said, "My impression is that the Rosary is of greatest value not only according to the words of Our Lady at Fatima, but according to the effects of the Rosary one sees throughout history. My impression is that Our Lady wanted to give ordinary people, who might not know how to pray, this simple method of getting closer to God."

From sinners to saints

We are all called to be holy. We are all called to be saints. God desires that we all be saved from our sins, have eternal life and live in union with him now and forever in heaven. He gives us free will and lets us decide what we want to do. The reason for free will is that God desires love, and love cannot exist without free choice. He could have programmed everyone to be loving, but then we'd be more like robots than persons. God desires to have a relationship with the persons he made us to be.

Even if we are living sinful lives, God loves us and wants us to come to Him. His mercy is greater than any sin we could ever commit or have committed. He desires us to come to him with a repentant heart, ask forgiveness, stop sinning with the help of his grace and to hold nothing back. He wants to forgive us, wipe out our sins and receive us to himself. He wants us to be happy with him forever.

No matter who we are or what we've done, God created each of us, loves us, wants to forgive our sins and to have a loving relationship with us. We might feel we aren't good enough for God. It's true that we aren't worthy of him, but he loves us anyway right now as we are. He desires us to be made perfect with his help. Grace gives us the ability and power to do what is right, and God gives it freely when we ask him for it.

God promises that his grace will be sufficient for us. We must not let our sins stop us from coming to God. Jesus is a bigger savior then we are a sinner, and he desires to save us. Jesus was born and died on the cross to save us from our sins so that we could have eternal life. We ask God for his help through prayer.

Helps us grow in love

St. Therese of Lisieux said that in the end, "It is love alone that counts." Loving God and others is what religion is all about and the reason we pray. Love is not only a feeling, even though feelings accompany it. Rather, love is both something we choose to do and a gift we accept from God.

We can't necessarily control our feelings, but we can control our will. Spontaneous feelings are not good or bad in a moral sense if they don't involve our will. They just are there making reports to us. We should recognize and identify them and then decide how we will choose to act. Having free will means that we can choose how we will act and choose to accept or reject God. We can choose to accept and act on God's grace to do what is right or we can reject God, refuse his graces and decide to sin. We can choose to love or to refuse to love. We can choose life or death, good or evil.

Truth is not relative or different for each person. Something is true and real regardless of what we think or feel about it. C.S. Lewis in *Mere Christianity* said, "Reality, in fact, is usually something you could not have guessed. That is one reason I believe Christianity. It is a religion you could not have guessed. If it offered us just the kind of universe we had always expected, I should feel we were making it up. But, in fact, it is not the sort of thing anyone would have made up. It has just that weird twist about it that real things have."

We wouldn't have guessed that God would become a man in the person of Jesus Christ. We wouldn't have guessed how much God loves us. We can't know completely what God has prepared for us in heaven. God's ways are very much above our ways. Jesus said, "I am the way, the truth and the life." (John 14:6) God reveals what is good and evil, and it's not necessarily the same as what "seems" right or "feels" good to us.

In his *Confessions*, St. Augustine said, "You have made us for yourself, and our hearts are restless until they find rest in You." When we love God above all else, we come to love everyone and everything worth loving all the more and in the proper proportions. Without this primary love for God, even the love we have for others or other things will fade. When we put first things first, (God), then secondary things, (such as people), are enhanced. God made us with a hole inside that only he can fill. If we try to fill it with other things, it doesn't work. Only God can fill this hole because it is God-sized.

Man, since his earliest beginnings, has sensed this. All civilizations have tried to define God or created their own gods or idols, to fill this God-hole inside. All attachments, however important they are to us, cannot take the place God has reserved for himself in our lives. In his infinite wisdom, God created us that only he, our Creator, can fill this hole.

Growing closer to Jesus

Jesus is God (the Son) and has been God for all of eternity along with God the Father and the Holy Spirit (one God in three Divine Persons). Jesus says if we love anything more than him we are not worthy of him. The most important thing we can do is to love God and put God first in our lives so that we do not miss out on our greatest good both now and forever, which is God. God is infinitely greater than anyone or anything else. Putting

God first means to love and choose God and his will above everything else, including ourselves.

Ultimately, if we gain God we have gained everything worth having because God not only gives us himself but everything else we need besides. (Matt 6:33.) In fact, God says in the Bible that as our Father, everything he has is ours. If we put anything above God we are not worthy to have God so we must ask God for the grace to love and value what is truly lovable (i.e. God) and to make it to heaven someday.

Besides learning all about God and his will through reading and pondering the Bible, and learning the official teachings of the Church as in the *Catechism*, we need to pray. Doing God's will and prayer are the main ways to grow in a loving personal relationship with God while here on earth. Praying the rosary or any heartfelt prayer helps us do that.

On Loving God

Our goal in the spiritual life is to love God more and more and to do his will. God is love and desires us to love him above all other people or things as he deserves to be loved. Jesus said if we love him we will keep his commandments.

Mary, our model

Mary is our model on how to love and follow God because she was so close to Jesus on earth and remains close in heaven. We don't pray to Mary in the same sense that we pray to God, but we ask Mary (and the Saints in heaven) for her help and prayers on our behalf, just as we often ask good people on earth for their help and prayers. Jesus desires that we love and honor his mother just as he loves and honors her. We are not only called to be children of God and to love God, but also to be members of God's family which includes having a relationship with Mary, the Saints in heaven, the souls in purgatory and all those in God's grace here on earth. This relationship is called the "communion of saints". The second greatest commandment is to love others as we love ourselves.

How does praying the rosary help us to love Jesus? It helps us in at least two ways. First, by meditating on events from the lives of Jesus and Mary, we come to know Jesus better. Secondly by opening our minds and hearts to Jesus, we allow him to speak to us in the depths of our being.

To love God we must know him

Before we can love God, we must first know him. Even though we can't see God with our eyes, we can come to know a lot about him and also to know him through having a personal relationship with him in prayer.

Besides prayer, we have at least three sources to learn about God so we can love and serve him better. The person of Jesus Christ and God's written word in the Bible are God's public revelation of himself to us. We can learn more about God through reading Scripture, and through the official teachings of the church such as the *Catechism of the Catholic Church*, Church documents and the popes' encyclicals. We have the Holy Spirit within us to enlighten and guide us. We can also learn more about God from the writings of his good friends, the Saints.

To realize the truth in our lives, besides just learning what is true, we need to put it into practice. If we do what Jesus tells us to do, we will know that it is true in the actual practice of doing what he says. Jesus says the person who puts his words into practice is like one who builds his house on rock, when the waves come the house will stand.

St. Jerome said that "ignorance of Scripture is ignorance of Christ" (*Jerome's Commentary on Isaiah*). We need to take time to read and reflect on Scripture especially regarding Jesus' life, and put the focus of our mind and heart on him. The rosary helps us to do this. Through prayer we come to know God better and grow closer, as prayer is the way we have a personal relationship with God.

Praying unceasingly

The Bible says, "Finally, brothers, whatever things are true, whatever things are honorable, whatever things are just, whatever things are pure, whatever things are lovely, whatever things are of good report; if there is any virtue, and if there is any praise, think about these things." (Phil. 4:8) To become like God, we must spend time thinking about him. Our goal is to keep our inner eye on God at all times as we go about our daily lives so that we are "pray without ceasing" (1 Ths. 5:17) as the Bible tells us to do. To pray always we become aware of God's presence within us, similar to how we are when our spouse, family members or a good friend are in the room with us. We sense their presence (and God's) even though we might not always be talking with them.

We can't spend all day speaking to God in vocal prayer, but in a sense we can pray always by remaining aware of God's presence with us as a constant companion as we go about our lives. Jesus said, "Whoever loves me will keep my word, and my Father will love him, and we will come to him and make our dwelling with him." (John 14:23) To pray unceasingly could include calling to mind that God is present with us as we go about our day, doing God's will in our daily duties and occasionally speaking to him (in either words, thoughts or sentiments) and also to spend dedicated quality time in prayer each day.

We are never really alone because God is always with us. If we desire to have a relationship with God, it's up to us to acknowledge his presence and respond to his love. He is always there waiting, but he doesn't force us. He just invites us.

Growing in the love of God

None of us loves God as much as he deserves to be loved, but our goal should be to grow in this love. As we begin to love God more, we will keep our thoughts and affections on him. We can compare this to an earthly example of when we fall in love with someone. We think about that person a lot, perhaps almost every moment. That person is always on our mind and in our heart.

Experiencing and becoming aware of God's great love for us fills our hearts with a joy, which goes beyond any earthly love or experience. If we open our hearts to God, he can fill us with his love and other gifts. We are made by and for God. We have a place inside our soul that only he can fill.

Growing in the love of God is the fruit of our prayer life, receiving the sacraments and doing God's will in our life. Through prayer, reflection on God's word in Scripture and doing what Jesus tells us to do, we come to know and love God more and more. After all, who could be more lovable or worthy of our focus than the most lovable, intelligent, powerful, Creator of the universe? He knows and loves us more than anyone else knows and loves us. His greatness is beyond our comprehension. If we love people, animals, the mountains, oceans or flowers, doesn't it make sense to love their Creator? If we love someone who loves us, wouldn't we want to love the One who made us and loves us more than anyone else?

This God who made the universe loves us and wants to have a personal love relationship with us. In fact, he wants to be our primary love relationship and attachment, and he deserves that in every way. He wants to fill us with his love and take care of all our needs. He wants to be not only our God and Father, but our constant companion and friend. He wants us to be happy with him forever. Religion is really all about love and relationship, loving God and our neighbor.

Loving God in our daily lives

When we finally realize how wonderful God is, we will want to learn everything possible about God. Just as we want to spend time with the people we love, so also we will want to spend time with God through prayer. We can't really say we have a loving relationship with someone if we don't take time to be with them. We make time for what is important to us. It follows that if God is important to us, or if we want him to become important, we will make time for him. If we want to love God, we will do what it takes to love him and develop a relationship with him. St. Teresa wrote in her autobiography (*Life* 8:5), "For mental prayer in my opinion is nothing else than an intimate sharing between friends; it means taking time frequently to be alone with him who we know loves us."

Union with God through prayer

Just as in human love where the lovers desire to be as united as possible, so in our love for God, unity is the goal, a unity of love and wills. If we desire to progress spiritually, we need to seek first and above all else to do God's will in all things. This leads to holiness and closeness to God. If we want what is best for ourselves and others, we already do want God's will because God alone knows what is really best. In desiring God's will, we desire what is best for ourselves and others. Wanting to do things our way is as limited as we are.

Despite how people love or refuse to love us, God is always waiting to have a relationship with us and wants to have as close as relationship as possible, to the point that he wants to give himself entirely to us. He asks that we give ourselves completely to him. The highest stage of spiritual development is often called spiritual marriage, or transforming union.

Jesus says, "Do not be afraid." Fear can be a temptation that holds us back. We can trust God who desires only what is best for us. When we give ourselves completely to God, he helps us to become the person he created us to be, our best self, for whatever vocation or plan he calls us. God has a different calling and plan for each person. When we give ourselves to God it may feel like we lose ourselves (Matt. 16:25), but in reality we become our true best selves in God.

If our goal is to love what deserves to be loved the most, God himself, we must first detach from the other things in our lives to the extent that they get in the way of loving God. If we desire to have a good relationship with God and straighten out our priorities, we will put God first in our lives. He will be on the throne of our lives.

An important part of making God a priority is to take time to pray each day. A husband may say he loves his wife, but if he never spends time with her or talks to her, one might begin to wonder how much he really loves her (or vice versa). Without communication, quality time and presence to each other, their relationship will deteriorate. There can't really be a relationship without relating. Prayer is something which is easy to neglect in our busy lives. But if we are serious about having a relationship with God, we need to find time to pray and make God and prayer a priority. In fact, we need to make God the center of our lives in all ways.

When we pray, things happen whether we realize it at that moment or not. The highest good to be gained is God himself, but in putting God first, God also gives us everything we need and ask for, as long as it will be truly good for us and is according to his plan. God sees us making the effort and he cannot be outdone in generosity. He reaches out to us more than we reach out to him. He communicates his secrets to us as we open our heart and mind to him.

Making Progress in Prayer

When we first pray as a meditation and/or conversation with God, it might seem that we are doing most of the talking. As we persevere in making the effort over time, our inner spiritual senses will become more attuned to God who will interject his thoughts and inspirations into our minds and hearts as we pay attention to him. If we experience God's action in our prayer, we can stop talking or meditating, and listen and experience what God is doing. As time goes on perhaps we will be almost unable to continue the vocal prayers of the rosary because our attention is being drawn to just be silent in God's presence and experience what God is doing. The Bible says, "Be still and know that I am God." This inability to meditate, when we would usually be able to, is one of three signs that God may be beginning to give us the gift of contemplation according to St. John of the Cross.

Transition from Meditation to Contemplation

St. John of the Cross' in *Ascent of Mt. Carmel* (Book 2, Chapter 13:1-4) gives us instructions on how to recognize the transition from meditation to contemplation.

He says, "The first sign is his realization that he can no longer meditate or reason with his imagination, neither can take pleasure therein as he was able to do before; he rather finds aridity in that which before would captivate his senses and to bring him sweetness. But, for as long as he finds sweetness in meditation, and is able to reason, he should not abandon this, save when his soul is led into the peace and quietness which is described under the third head." (See the third sign below.)

"The second sign is a realization that he has no desire to fix his mediation or his sense upon other particular objects, exterior or interior. I do not mean that the imagination neither comes nor goes (for even at times of deep recollection it is apt to move freely), but that the soul has no pleasure in fixing it of set purpose upon other objects.

"The third and surest sign is that the soul takes pleasure in being alone, and waits with loving attentiveness upon God, without making any particular meditation, in inward peace and quietness and rest, and without its own acts and exercises of the faculties — memory, understanding and will...

"The spiritual person must observe all of these three signs together in himself, before he can safely abandon meditation and sense, and enter that of contemplation and spirit."

St. John of the Cross gives us an indication of when meditation is to be set aside for contemplation. (He mentions also that unless we have begun to experience this we may not understand. So until such a time as we do understand, we can keep meditating and leave it up to God.)

St. Teresa of Avila also has a lot to say about this as well. Her instructions are that we are to remain receptive if God grants us this gift of infused contemplation. But she also says that if God does not grant this, then we are not to sit there for extended periods doing nothing, trying to force something to happen. Instead we are to pray or meditate actively as we can while being attentive to any communications from God. If the Lord takes the initiative, then we remain receptive to what he is giving while he gives it. If not, we pray as we can.

In her book, *Interior Castle*, Fourth Mansions, Chapter 3, St. Teresa's explains, "What we have to do is to beg like poor and needy persons coming before a great and rich Emperor and then cast down our eyes in humble expectation. When from the secret signs he gives us we seem to realize that he is hearing us, it is well for us to keep silence, since he has permitted us to be near him and there will be no harm in our striving not to labour with the understanding – provided, I mean, that we are able to do so. But if we are not quite sure that the King has heard us, or sees us, we must not stay where we are like ninnies, for there still remains a great deal for the soul to do when it has stilled the understanding; if it did nothing more it would experience much greater aridity and the imagination would grow more restless because of the effort caused it by cessation from thought...

"The second reason is that all these interior activities are gentle and peaceful, and to do anything painful brings us harm rather than help. By 'anything painful' I mean anything that we try to force ourselves to do; it would be painful, for example, to hold our breath. The soul must just leave itself in the hands of God, and do what he wills it to do, completely disregarding its own advantage and resigning itself as much as it possibly can to the will of God.

"The third reason is that the very effort which the soul makes in order to cease from thought will perhaps awaken thought and cause it to think a great deal.

"The fourth reason is that the most important and pleasing thing in God's eyes is our remembering His honour and glory and forgetting ourselves and our own profit and ease and pleasure. And how can a person be forgetful of himself when he is taking such great care about his actions that he dare not even stir, or allow his understanding and desires to stir, even for the purpose of desiring the greater glory of God or of rejoicing in the glory which is his? When his Majesty wishes the working of the understanding to cease, he employs it in another manner, and illumines the soul's knowledge to so much higher a degree than any we can ourselves attain that he leads it into a state of absorption, in which, without knowing how, it is much better instructed than it could ever be as a result of its own efforts, which would only spoil everything. God gave us our faculties to work with, and everything will have its due reward; there is no reason, then, for trying to cast a spell over them – they must be allowed to perform their office until God gives them a better one."

St. Teresa tells us that contemplation isn't brought about by a certain technique. Rather it is a gift that God grants when and if he wills. If there is something we can do to dispose ourselves to receive this gift, it would be to be faithful to God in prayer, loving him above all things and doing his will. In this way, contemplation is more a result of focusing on God in a self-forgetful way than focusing on prayer techniques, such as trying to keep our minds empty or other such things.

Following God's lead

So the advice is to keep praying in a way that we can and to follow God's lead. While praying, God will enlighten us more and more. If we notice the Lord initiating something, we will want to pay attention. We don't want to miss or dismiss God's communications to us. If we have a set time for prayer and our time is used up praying contemplatively, and we didn't finish our rosary or other prayers, we have prayed well. The goal of prayer is union with God, not to finish a set amount of prayers. When and if God decides to initiate, our job is to remain receptive rather than trying to force ourselves to meditate or finish vocal prayers. (An exception to this may be obligatory prayers like the Office for religious.)

When we give ourselves to God, God gives us what we need at each moment to become the person he wants us to be. The Bible says we are all sinners and have fallen short of the glory of God (Rom. 3:23). But God calls us to be made perfect with the help of his grace.

Dry times in prayer

Besides the times in prayer when God seems so close, there are also times when God seems to be silent. Dry times at prayer are part of our growth as well. If God seems to remain silent or prayer seems dry, God is calling us all the more to make the effort to persevere in prayer, whether it be just sitting there in his presence or actively meditating.

We might also want to reexamine ourselves to see if we are putting God first in our lives. We can't serve both God and mammon at the same time. (Matt 6:24)

Consolations in prayer are great joys but we are to seek the God of joy, and not the joys of God. It is a subtle distinction but the dry times reveal our intent. If we seek only good feelings we will give up prayer when we don't feel something. If we seek God, we will discipline ourselves (with the help of grace) to do God's will over our own comfort. It is a battle against our own will, but just as we often have to force ourselves to exercise our bodies to be in shape, so we need to discipline ourselves to be in spiritual shape.

God desires that we grow in virtue and holiness. There is also spiritual warfare which means the devil struggles against us when we try to do good. God is in control and only allows what will ultimately be good for us and our sanctification.

A desert-like experience can also accompany contemplative prayer. We may experience purifying action to get us ready to be united with God in a more profound way. We need to be purified from our sins and inordinate attachments in this life or the next before we are ready for union with God.

Determination to persevere

The important thing is to persevere and seek God above all else. St. John of the Cross instructs us to live by faith alone. He tells us to focus on the honor and glory of God rather than on spiritual experiences. He says not to pay much attention to spiritual experiences: if these are from God, they will have their good effect, and if they are not from God, they can mislead us. If we do what faith demands, we will continue (with the help of grace) to get closer to God. We will form habits that make prayer and serving God easier and a delight over time. God has the capacity to be our greatest happiness, for who is like God? If we have God and remain in his grace, he will give us everything we need besides. If we don't have God, nothing else will completely satisfy us, because we don't have the ultimate good who is God.

Initially, and maybe for years, prayer may seem like an effort on our part. Be assured that even if we don't feel anything, things are happening when we make the effort to pray and be in communion with God. God often works secretly within and reveals his work at some future date to show us what he has been doing all at once.

One last thought, the way we can tell if we are praying well is if we are growing in virtue over time. We might not be able to see our relationship with God, but the sign of growth, according to St. Teresa of Avila, is an increase in love of our neighbor. She says that love of neighbor, detachment and humility (teachability) are what we need most to grow.

A Biblical Prayer

The prayers of the rosary are mainly derived from Scripture. The Our Father is the prayer that Jesus taught us as recorded in Matthew 6:5-13: "When you pray, you shall not be as the hypocrites, for they love to stand and pray in the synagogues and in the corners of the streets, that they may be seen by men. Most certainly, I tell you, they have received their reward. But you, when you pray, enter into your inner chamber, and having shut your door, pray to your Father who is in secret, and your Father who sees in secret will reward you openly. In praying, don't use vain repetitions, as the Gentiles do; for they think that they will be heard for their much speaking. Therefore don't be like them, for your Father knows what things you need, before you ask him. Pray like this: 'Our Father in heaven, may your name be kept holy. Let your Kingdom come. Let your will be done, as in heaven, so on earth. Give us today our daily bread. Forgive us our debts, as we also forgive our debtors. Bring us not into temptation, but deliver us from the evil one.'"

The quote above talks about "vain repetitions" which is sometimes misunderstood to mean that Jesus was speaking against using repetition in prayer. However the Bible itself says that Jesus himself prayed repetitiously, saying the same words repeatedly in the Garden of Gethsemani before he was arrested (Matt 26: 36-44). So it is not repetition that Jesus is speaking against but "vain" repetition.

Since prayer is a lifting of one's heart and mind to God, it seems that repeating the same prayers would be appropriate to express the same thoughts and affections.

They would not be "vain" if one is truly prayerful. Besides, the Bible says to "pray unceasingly". One need not reinvent something new to say each moment or each prayer time.

The Hail Mary is also a prayer that is mainly derived from Scripture. The first part is taken from Luke 1:28, where the Angel Gabriel announced to Mary that she had been chosen to be the mother of the Messiah. "Having come in, the angel said to her, 'Rejoice, you highly favored one! The Lord is with you. Blessed are you among women!'"

In Luke 1:42, we have the second sentence of the Hail Mary. The Angel Gabriel also told Mary that her cousin, Elizabeth, was expecting. Mary went to visit Elizabeth. Upon her arrival, "It happened, when Elizabeth heard Mary's greeting, that the baby leaped in her womb, and Elizabeth was filled with the Holy Spirit. She called out with a loud voice, and said, 'Blessed are you among women, and blessed is the fruit of your womb!' "

Besides the prayers of the rosary coming mainly from Scripture, the mysteries of the rosary themselves are mainly important events taken from the Gospels, as you can see by the Scriptural quotations for the mysteries in this book.

The idea of honoring Mary is also Scriptural as seen in Luke 1:46-48: "And Mary said: My soul doth magnify the Lord. And my spirit hath rejoiced in God my Saviour. Because he hath regarded the humility of his handmaid: for behold from henceforth all generations shall call me blessed."

The Family Rosary

Saying the family rosary can be a challenge, but it can also become a special time for the whole family including the children. Following are some ideas that have worked for my family that you might want to try.

First of all, set a usual time that is best for everyone (not during favorite shows or activities). A good time might be right before the children's usual bedtime or consider extending their bedtime by 20 minutes (the usual time it takes to say the rosary). One idea is to give the children a choice of going to bed at the usual time or staying up an extra 20 minutes to say the family rosary. That way they feel they get to do something special that they wouldn't ordinarily get to do and they are already winding down for the night. It's a good idea to get each child their own rosary and perhaps a small pamphlet with pictures of the mysteries of the rosary. If your children like to make things, you might want to make your own rosaries. Materials for making rosaries are available on the web. For small children you can even make or buy rosaries with big beads.

One idea to get the children's attention and keep them focused, is to wait until it gets dark to say the rosary and then turn off most or all of the lights. Have a special candle to use while saying the rosary, and let one of the children light the candle. Let the children take turns lighting the candle before beginning the rosary and blowing it out at the end of the rosary. If the room is dark or semi-dark it helps the children to be quiet and not to get distracted. (Don't forget to put the matches in a safe place.) Lighting the candle and prayer can become a family event of shared closeness with each other and God.

Another idea is to let the children take turns leading the decades if they are old enough and to let them each add their own intentions before beginning the rosary. If some children really do not want to join in, especially teenagers, it might be a good idea just to invite them and give them a choice, rather than forcing them. Parents often have a sense of when a little pressure will be good or when it is counterproductive.

Another idea is that little children (who often can't pay attention very long) or even busy teenagers could be encouraged to say one decade and then be allowed to leave after that if they choose. The goal is to encourage them to want prayer as part of their life and to associate prayer with a positive experience and not to associate it with punishment or negative interactions. If they see the lights off, the candle burning and everyone else praying, this often pulls them in to want to be included.

Teenagers often have serious concerns. Offering to say the rosary for their special intentions may encourage them to want to be a part of the family rosary. Since they are at a time in their life where they are becoming adults, it is important to let them make more of their own decisions. Inviting rather than forcing becomes more important for older children. Bribing is not recommended as a way to get children to pray! We don't want them to think they only do good things if there is something extra in it for them. We want them to learn that praying, like virtue, "is its own reward".

Also it is possible to obtain a plenary indulgence for oneself or a soul in purgatory when saying a family rosary, under the usual conditions. More information about this can be seen in the *Enchiridion of Indulgences* which is online at the Vatican website at *www.vatican.va*.

The Fatima Message

"Pray the Rosary every day in honor of Our Lady of the Rosary to obtain peace in the world."
Our Lady of Fatima, July 13, 1917

"Pray much and make sacrifices for sinners, for many souls go to hell because there is no one to make sacrifices for them." *Our Lady of Fatima, August 19, 1917*

"Sacrifice yourselves for sinners and say often whenever you make a sacrifice: 'O Jesus, it is for love of You, for the conversion of sinners, and in reparation for the offenses committed against the Immaculate Heart of Mary.' "
Our Lady of Fatima, July 13, 1917

Lucia, one of the Fatima seers, said: "Many persons feeling that the word penance implies great austerities, and not feeling that they have the strength for great sacrifices, become discouraged and continue a life of lukewarmness and sin." She said Jesus told her: "The sacrifice required of every person is the fulfillment of his duties in life and the observance of My law. This is the penance that I now seek and require."

"My impression is that Our Lady wanted to give ordinary people, who might not know how to pray, this simple method of getting closer to God." *Sr. Lucia of Fatima*

The Fifteen Promises of the Rosary

Our Blessed Mother made the following promises to those who pray the Rosary faithfully:

1. To all those who shall pray my Rosary devoutly, I promise my special protection and great graces.

2. Those who shall persevere in the recitation of my Rosary will receive some special grace.

3. The Rosary will be a very powerful armor against hell; it will destroy vice, deliver from sin and dispel heresy.

4. The rosary will make virtue and good works flourish, and will obtain for souls the most abundant divine mercies. It will draw the hearts of men from the love of the world and its vanities, and will lift them to the desire of eternal things. Oh, that souls would sanctify themselves by this means.

5. Those who trust themselves to me through the Rosary will not perish.

6. Whoever recites my Rosary devoutly reflecting on the mysteries, shall never be overwhelmed by misfortune. He will not experience the anger of God nor will he perish by an unprovided death. The sinner will be converted; the just will persevere in grace and merit eternal life.

7. Those truly devoted to my Rosary shall not die without the sacraments of the Church.

8. Those who are faithful to recite my Rosary shall have during their life and at their death the light of God and the plenitude of His graces and will share in the merits of the blessed.

9. I will deliver promptly from purgatory souls devoted to my Rosary.

10. True children of my Rosary will enjoy great glory in heaven.

11. What you shall ask through my Rosary you shall obtain.

12. To those who propagate my Rosary I promise aid in all their necessities.

13. I have obtained from my Son that all the members of the Rosary Confraternity shall have as their intercessors, in life and in death, the entire celestial court.

14. Those who recite my Rosary faithfully are my beloved children, the brothers and sisters of Jesus Christ.

15. Devotion to my Rosary is a special sign of predestination.

The above promises were given in private revelation to Saint Dominic and Blessed Alan.

About the Author

Kathryn Marcellino is a Roman Catholic and a member of the Secular Order of Discalced Carmelites (OCDS). She has experience teaching formation lessons on Carmelite spirituality. She is also a spiritual director, having received her training in spiritual direction from the Diocese of Stockton School of Ministries and The Mercy Center in Burlingame, California. She is married to Dennis Marcellino, who is an author, speaker and musician, and is the mother of five children.

Kathryn offers spiritual direction through e-mail and answers to questions on the Catholic faith through her web site at *www.CatholicSpiritualDirection.org*. Her website also has general spiritual direction from the teachings of the Church and the writings of the saints through articles and links.

Printed in the United States
105986LV00001B/179/A

9 780945 272267